ART DECO
FASHION AND JEWELRY

ART DECO FASHION AND JEWELRY

CHARTWELL
BOOKS, INC.

Published by Chartwell Books
A Division of Book Sales Inc.
114 Northfield Avenue
Edison, New Jersey 08837
USA

Copyright ©1998 Quantum Books Ltd

0-7858-0987-2

This book is produced by
Quantum Books Ltd
6 Blundell Street
London N7 9BH

Project Manager: Rebecca Kingsley
Project Editor: Judith Millidge
Designer: Wayne Humphries
Editor: Clare Haworth-Maden

The material in this publication previously appeared in
*Art Deco Source Book, Art Deco: An Illustrated Guide to
the Decorative Style, Encyclopedia of Art Deco, Art Deco:
An Illustrated Guide, 20s & 30s Style, The Decorative Arts
Library: Jewelry*

QUMADJM
Set in Times
Reproduced in Singapore by United Graphic Ltd
Printed in Singapore by Star Standard Industries (Pte) Ltd

CONTENTS

AN INTRODUCTION TO ART DECO

Art Deco survives today as the last truly sumptuous style, an extremely fertile chapter in the history of the applied arts. Art Deco is essentially a style used for the applied arts, though most of its sources are in the fine arts, architecture, as well as sculpture and painting. It was the first truly twentieth-century style which was international. Arriving when it did, it was a style that could be adapted to every man-made object. It also arrived at a time when new forms of communication would ensure its rapid spread. Finally, and most importantly, it was the last total style.

The term "Art Deco," which derives from the Exposition des Arts Décoratifs et Industriels, held in Paris in 1925, is used to describe, in somewhat simplified terms, the many diverse developments that took place in the world of design between the two wars. It is, however, an apt title for the artistic style that followed on immediately from Art Nouveau at the end of the nineteenth century. The latter had relied on floral motifs to pattern and ornament its artifacts, whereas Art Deco was thoroughly modern in turning away from the winding, sinuous qualities of Art Nouveau, looking instead to those of abstract design and color for

Above: A hand-tinted postcard advertising the 1925 Exposition Internationale des Arts Décoratifs et Industriels in Paris.

Opposite: An American powder compact decorated with a handsome geometric motif dating from the late 1930s.

MINISTÈRE DU COMMERCE ET DE L'INDUSTRIE

PARIS-1925

EXPOSITION
INTERNATIONALE
DES ARTS DÉCORATIFS
ET INDUSTRIELS
MODERNES
AVRIL- OCTOBRE

IMPRIMERIE DE VAUGIRARD, PARIS

color's sake; and, when turning to nature for inspiration, it preferred to portray animals, or the beauties of the female form. Where Art Nouveau had been heavy, complex and crowded, Art Deco was clean and pure. The lines in Art Deco did not swirl around like the center of a whirlpool; if they curved, they were gradual and sweeping, following a fine arc; if they were straight, they were straight as a ruler. Art Deco could be light-hearted on one level and deadly serious and practical on another. As the style in a time of unprecedented change, it was fluid enough to reflect that change.

THE ORIGINS OF ART DECO

The style which later became known as Art Deco traces its origins to the period before World War I. In the first decade of the twentieth century, many factors caused an abrupt change in fashion. The couturier Paul Poiret, for example, revolutionized dress design, freeing the female form from constricting layers of clothing. Serge Diaghilev's performances of the Ballets Russes in Paris in 1909 and in the United States in 1916 provided another influence, both through their introduction of bright colors into the drab world of fashion, and their emphasis on the Orient. New art movements, such as Cubism, Futurism and neo-plasticism, helped further to create a new vernacular for art, which in turn initiated new concepts in jewelry design that were taken up with renewed interest after World War I.

A MODERN STYLE

The spirit of Art Deco was the spirit of the modern. Even though it adapted older styles for its own use, it was still the style of the

Left: A French poster designed for the 1925 Paris Exposition by Robert Bonfils.

new. It was the style of the age that wouldn't stay still and looked to that age for its content, its meaning and often its subject matter. Art Deco may have been the modern style, but it emerged from as many different directions as it had applications. Art Deco was given its greatest cohesion in the Exposition of 1925, in a city that was also the Paris of Pablo Picasso, Georges Braque, Fernand Léger ad Robert and Sonia Delauney. Such Art Deco pieces as a decorated cigarette lighter by Gérard Sandoz could not have come from any time earlier than 1910.

THE PARISIAN INFLUENCE
Paris was the stage on which almost all the battles of modern art were fought. The rapidity with which style has since followed on style has made it almost impossible to discern any lasting direction today. From Impressionism through post-Impressionism, Symbolism, Cubism, Futurism, Orphism, Constructivism, Purism, Surrealism, Vorticism, one "ism" has replaced the next with disarming regularity.

THE TREND TOWARD ABSTRACTION
What many of these "isms" had in common, which would be of great importance to Art Deco, was that they shared a tendency toward abstraction, moving away from more obvious subject matter towards a concern for the basic elements of picture-making or sculpting, so that form, color, line and volume became important in themselves. The artist's feelings and sensibility could be read, it was hoped, through the manipulation of those infinitely flexible variables. As for the decorative arts

Right: The fantastically popular Josephine Baker adopts one of the exaggerated poses that were popular with Art Deco sculptors.

Far right: An ivory and bronze bust by an anonymous sculptor. The subject wears an elaborately decorated cloche hat.

Right: This enameled metal powder compact is a souvenir of the Empire State Building and dates from the 1930s.

in the Art Deco style, they ranged from the purely functional, through simple and clear decoration, to pure ornament. That is why it is impossible to talk of one Art Deco style: there were as many directions, hybrids and strains as there were practitioners. The easiest way to understand and unravel the puzzle is to see where Art Deco came from and what sources it may have used.

THE EMERGENCE OF THE AVANT-GARDE

When Picasso and Braque set off together in 1907 on the journey through their radical discoveries that would lead to Cubism, they turned art, as it had then been understood, on its head. The shock waves pulsed across Europe into

Russia, and across to North America in less than five years. Out of Picasso, abstraction had been born. The process of art had become a search, an experiment. Modernism came into being, and the avant-garde was invented. It had become viable, and ultimately necessary, to test out all the infinite options, to play intellectual games, and to extend and expand the boundaries of art. To be ahead of one's time, or at least up there with it, pushing forward, was to be a modernist. Like-minded designers could apply these principles to the decorative arts and arrive at something wholly novel. In a lesser way, they could apply the color schemes of a Mondrian painting, a Goncharova, El Lissitzky, a Wyndham Lewis, or simpler

still, a Malevich, and arrive at simplicity itself. In the transition from fine art to applied art, the most simple motif had passed from being shocking, avant-garde and bewildering, to being accepted and merely decorative.

ART NOUVEAU AND PRIMITIVE ART

Art Nouveau was of central importance to the rise of Art Deco, if only as a style to react against. Equally, Hoffman, Olbrich, Peche and Moser, who founded the Wiener Werkstätte at the beginning of the century, were early practitioners of a style which, when refined, looked like very early Art Deco. Another influence, which probably became the most important of all, was a response to primitive art. What had happened throughout the late nineteenth century was a reappraisal of primitive art. Anything that was not European was recognized as having some artistic worth. Indeed, Europe looked away from the products of a diseased society that had chosen to massacre its youth across the battlefields of the Somme, to an art that was primitive, untouched and natural. This was particularly relevant to Art Deco, because by the time the style began to develop, a tendency toward the primitive was not just an option, it was obligatory.

THE BALLETS RUSSES

Nobody looking back at Paris in the first quarter of this century could ignore the impact of the Ballets Russes on the arts. Driven by its passionate Svengali and impresario, Serge Diaghilev, its stage designs and costumes mixed the Oriental with the Westernized, the avant-garde with the primitive. Léon Bakst, its most famous designer, produced costumes whose lavishness and exotic Orientalism came as a complete shock to the Parisian public. Diaghilev's production of *Scheherezade* was a riot of deep, rich color, which would inspire the heavier, decorative side of Art Deco and interior design.

ERTÉ'S SET DESIGNS

Even more ambitious in the Art Deco style were the thousands of gouache drawings for set designs of Erté. The sinuous, sweeping curves of dresses and curtains fell across a rigidly simple, but still evocative, backdrop. Elegantly arched windows looked in on novel interiors bedecked with leopard-skin rugs and abstract, rectilinear furniture, enlivened by

Right: La Naissance d'Aphrodite, *a Cubist interpretation by Paul Véra, 1925.*

Right: For the Voice, *a strong Constructivist image by the Russian artist El Lissitzky.*

Below: Pearls, and Things and Palm Beach, *a watercolor by Emil J Bisttram.*

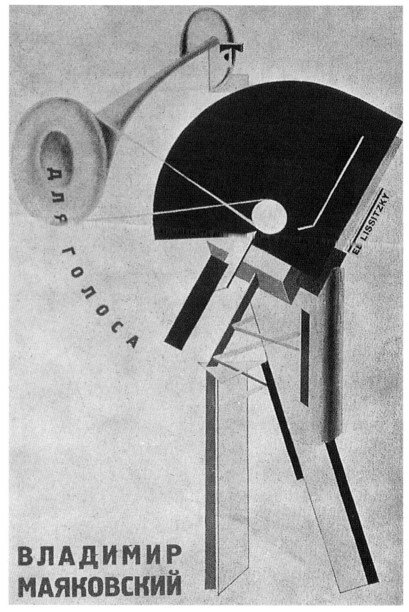

dancers in Oriental costume. That was part of Diaghilev's legacy to Art Deco. If that was not enough, he also incorporated the latest in contemporary dance, design and music.

If Oriental art had been made fashionable by the Ballets Russes, Mexican, Egyptian, North American Indian and South American art was of equal importance. What Art Deco learned, and then taught the public, was bold design. If colors were to be bright, they should knock you over; if lines were to be clear, they should be as stark and severe as the steps up a temple. The obvious could be chic. Indeed, if any one trend could be said to characterize the 1920s and 1930s it must be the way in which innovation was constantly and rapidly transmuted into chic. The radical tendencies and advances in art, architecture and design were fast subsumed into the broad arena of public consumption, into such disparate and far-flung areas as transportation, politics and mass communication.

THE AFTERMATH OF WORLD WAR I

Prior to these two decades, the West had been effectively destroyed by World War I. But cataclysm became a catalyst for fundamental change: in the postwar world the desire for a fresh start, for a new epoch of progress and peace, became paramount. By the 1920s the world had changed politically. In Germany, the founding of the Weimar Republic in 1919 created a climate in which an institution such as the Bauhaus could operate. In Russia, the founding of the Union of Soviet Socialist Republics also had its repercussions on a worldwide scale. Later still, in Italy and Germany, the rise of

Right: An English enamelled silver cigarette case, 1931. The dancing couple wears loose, Oriental-style costumes.

Right: The exotic costume design by Romain de Tirtoff (Erté) for the character Assad in the ballet Dance de Jouet, *from* One Thousand and One Nights.

fascism was set in opposition to communist ideas. The world economic recession, the great slump and the Wall Street Crash contributed to the political and economic cocktail which helped to create the unique character of the Art Deco decades.

These were also truly international decades, for great international exhibitions (such as the 1925 Art Deco exhibition in Paris) at once aided the flow of ideas between continents, while paradoxically shoring up nationalist tendencies. Once every four years the Olympics performed the same functions, showing the world national displays and international cooperation.

World War I acted as a catalyst in other ways, too. The industrial world made advances far beyond those which would have been occasioned by five years of peace time. Aeronautics, medicine and industrial chemistry benefited from the effects of the "war to end all wars." Industry itself had found that it needed to develop extremely efficient mass-production techniques in order to cope with demand.

THE MACHINE AGE

So the final, and one of the most obvious, influences on Art Deco was there to see at every street corner, in every house, factory and store, on the sea, and also in the air. The twentieth century was the machine age. Art Deco was modern because it used aspects of machine design as inspiration: the wings of an airplane, the bow of a yacht, the porthole of the cabin window of the new ocean liners, the cogs and wheels of a sewing machine or an automobile engine. It was even more modern because

Right: An African couple drawn by George Barbier in 1920. The lush exoticism of Africa appealed to Art Deco designers, as did the delicate ornamentation of Asia.

Below: This detail of a Philadelphia diner illustrates how architects took the materials and forms of the industrial age and magnified them to architectural proportions.

NEW YORK DIRECT
O QUEBEC & MONTREAL

it accelerated the adoption of new materials such as plastic, Bakelite and chrome. And, while Art Deco upheld the importance of crafts-manship in the teeth of the new forms of mass production, it often benefited greatly from this development. Although Art Deco objects were originally made with expensive and rare materials, many ideas were copied and man-ufactured to provide cheaper alternatives for the less wealthy public.

AN ALL-PERVASIVE STYLE

Art Deco was therefore a style that spread through every aspect of daily life between the wars; every form of art and craft used the new sensibility, as is particularly reflected in the worlds of jewelry and fashion that are explored in this book.

Above: Two of Cunard's most famous liners, the Queen Mary *and* Queen Elizabeth, *illustrated in Art Deco style in a poster dating from the 1950s.*

ART DECO
FASHION

The world of fashion, clothing and accessories is always quick to pick up on the latest changes in taste. The fashion that appeared during the 1920s and 1930s is well known to anyone who has ever looked at movies of the period, and it is not difficult to build up an accurate, if superficial, overview of fashion during the 1920s and 1930s from the statuettes by Preiss, the photograph of Nancy Cunard in her African bangles, or photographs of Picasso, Jean Cocteau and others *flâneurs* and *poseurs*. Art Deco fashion has been repeated and diluted so many times since that it becomes difficult to place it historically, to see where it came from, or to notice how subtle modifications point to a dress being a 1960s' replica or the original.

Right: Match de Boxe (Boxing Match), *a fashion plate that appeared in the influential French fashion journal* Art, Goût, Beauté *in May 1923.*

The reason for the rapid success of Art Deco was that it was essentially a fashionable style. All styles have their day, but in the twentieth century the fashion industry moved quicker in response to public taste than ever before. This has as much to do with built-in obsolescence as with a sense of style and finesse; both feed off each other. Tastes fluctuate quickly, so the industry has to come up with something new, as clients try to stay one step ahead of the rest of the pack. Then, as now, styles changed from season to season, with hemlines constantly fluctuating, waistlines appearing and disappearing, skirts growing slimmer or fuller. None the less, the great early Paris couturiers dramatically brought fashion to the fore, making it as influential as any other design medium, a circumstance that has remained constant in the six or seven decades since they first made their mark.

Preceding page: Portrait of Nancy Cunard by the society photographer Cecil Beaton.

In itself, fashion may only be as important to people as the amount of care they take in clothing themselves. For the elegant Parisian or New Yorker of the 1920s and 1930s, fashion was a vital part of life. Fashion is always to do with snobbishness, and with Art Deco this was particularly important, since it was a total style. If your collector lived amongst Ruhlmann tables, Lalique sculptures, African chairs by Pierre Legrain, lights by Brandt and Daum, a coffee service by Sèvres or Clarice Cliff, place settings by Jean Puiforcat; if he or she lit your cigarette with a lighter designed

Right: A poster by Paul Colin advertising the Revue Nègre that was then all the rage.

Below: A 1922 drawing from Art, Goût, Beauté *of a model wearing a white crêpe cocktail dress by Worth.*

Right: Kora, *a gilt- and gold-painted bronze and ivory figure of an exotic dancer by Demetre Chiparus.*

by Gérard Sandoz to the strains of Paul Robeson or a jazz number on the gramophone, then you could guarantee that the cut of the husband's suit, the length and sharpness of his lapels, the width of necktie and the wife's dress by Schiaparelli would be precisely in keeping. If so much effort in intellect, taste and money had been expended on creating the home environment, then the only things that could travel out of the door (clothes and jewelry) had to be just as important; they had to complement the overall effect.

THE STYLE OF THE AGE

There is a somewhat perverse rule in fashion that the poorer the economic climate for the majority of people, the more ostentatious the select, wealthy few become. The double standards of the "Roaring Twenties," in the United States particularly, where Prohibition cast a depressing cloud of double-dealing, suspicion and crime, reflected itself in the androgynous short skirts, bob cuts and shapeless tops worn by the flappers. By the beginning of the 1930s, when the reality was far more depressing and the comforting stool of wealth had been kicked away from under the feet of the erstwhile bootleggers, the fashion became fuller, while the jewelry (even if it was paste) became even more startling.

Fashion played a very important role in Art Deco design, not only in terms of its direct influence on other mediums (the Ballets Russes costumes, for instance, made waves) but also because many of its leading lights, Paul Poiret, Jacques Doucet and Jeanne Lanvin among them, were extraordinary collectors and tastemakers who helped enormously to promote *Le Style 25.* In terms of design, the effect of fashion items on the other applications of Art Deco was fairly minimal; as a mirror to hold

L'Asie

Far left: Asian fashion as interpreted by George Barbier in an illustration dating from 1920.

Left: This Barbier stencil from La Gazette du Bon Ton *shows a dancer in a low-waisted dress. The cap was a typical head-covering of the day.*

up and see the speed of change reflected, however, fashion was unrivaled. Sometimes, of course, the converse was true. The statuettes and Chryselephantine figures of Otto Poerzl and Ferdinand Preiss were direct reflections of the opera and ballet costumes, as well as the ballroom clothes, of the period. They were knowing little nods; small, elegant gestures of recognition that the owner appreciated the essence of what it was to be fashionable.

FASHION ILLUSTRATION

Fashion illustration was significant as well: for not only did the drawings of Paul Iribe, Georges Lepape, George Barbier and Erté help in themselves to spread the new couture, but furthermore, their styles and use of vivid colors had a strong influence on many other artists

in France and across the world.

In Parisian fashion design, as in other mediums, the influence of the Ballets Russes was paramount. Serge Diaghilev's company had invaded the French capital in 1909, and its Oriental splendor – in costumes, scenery and dance itself – transformed the course of Gallic design. Almost immediately, Léon Bakst's exotic creations, his ornamental, brightly hued and sumptuous fabrics, began to be reflected in French couture. Color, which had before been reduced to subdued shades in clothing, suddenly came alive with the Ballets Russes. Bakst's sets, and costumes radiated with oranges, bright blues and greens, generating a sudden craze for anything Eastern.

At the same time the impact of Paul Poiret (1879–1944) was being felt as he brought this

mania for the exotic into fashion, first by streamlining dresses and then by introducing the Empire waistline. Having started his career working for both Worth and Doucet, he had already begun to make his name by 1906, with his fluid dress designs distinguished by their smooth, corsetless line, which in effect liberated twentieth-century woman from the past. In 1908, Paul Iribe had produced a set of vividly colored *pochoirs* (that is, stenciled ink drawings) illustrating his new fashions, *Les Robes de Paul Poiret*. The bright colors and exotic, Oriental aspects of his fashions derived from his love of Indian and Persian art and his admiration for the Ballets Russes. His vivid creations, coupled with those of the Ballets Russes, heralded a new era, not only in design but in illustration as well. Preceding most of Art Deco by at least a decade, they were very much in the forefront of the style.

PAUL POIRET

Paul Poiret spread his influence and taste far wider than most of the other French fashion designers, for he was not only a dress designer. Indeed, he advanced the entire style with the workshop he founded in 1912, the Atelier Martine (named after his daughter), where he employed young working-class girls whose charming drawings and designs were the basis for rugs and carpets, upholstery and drape fabrics, wallpapers, furniture, lamps, and even dolls, which he marketed through his Maison Martine. Whole interior-design schemes were the products of Poiret and his atelier, not only for his own residences but also for those of others. At the Exposition des Arts Décoratifs et Industriels Poiret exhibited his designs on decorated barges just under the Alexander III bridge. He was, above all, a patron of the arts and a man of true Art Deco taste, supporting young artists and also collecting their works, creating perfumes, publishing books, and holding fancy costume balls. When he needed an architect for his fashion house in Paris, he used the firm of Perret Frères. The entrance door to the premises was one of Edgar Brandt's masterpieces in metalwork. Poiret recognized the importance of creating a suitable environment in which to display his talents and impress his wealthy clientele.

THE CHANGING ROLE OF WOMEN

World War I introduced women into the workforce, helping to liberate them further from constrictive clothing. For patriotic reasons, it became acceptable for women to undertake certain types of work previously barred to them. This change in the traditional role of

Above: A Hindustan design by Paul Poiret from the Gazette du Bon Ton, *1920.*

women brought a sweeping transformation in what they wore. Furthermore, during World War I there was a need to conserve heavy fabrics for the troops, which hastened women's acceptance of a softer, slimmer silhouette. In 1917, Mrs. Vernon Castle arrived in Paris and changed forever the concept of the ideal woman. Her slim, lithe figure glided across the dance floor, charming society with the latest ballroom dances and providing a preview of the energetic woman who appeared after the war to challenge the staidness of her predecessor's role in society. By the time the war ended in 1918, women had gained freedom in dress and were not about to give it up.

Poiret's slim, high-waisted dresses had been replaced in 1917 with a line of low-waisted models. Besides the straight, sleek, sometimes Empire-waisted dresses which liberated the Art Deco woman from painful corsets and bulky petticoats, she could be seen wearing exotic turbans, often bejeweled or plumed, small cloche hats and bandeaux perched above her eyebrows.

THE NEW FASHIONS

By the end of World War I, hems were almost universally short (but still below the knee), and waists began to be dropped. Busts were deemphasized, and backless dresses – declarations of freedom – abounded for evening. Colors were bright, often outrageously so, and patterns were bold, usually floral. Their hairstyles also reflected women's new, postwar independence, becoming short and cropped or "bobbed." Hemlines fluctuated for the first five years of the 1920s, from ankle to calf length. Then, in 1925, skirt hems shot up to just below the knee (the length associated with the 1920s today), and dropped back to mid-calf length in 1929. The silhouette of the body became long and flat and suppressed all curves. Both the neckline and the back of the dress fluctuated, the latter plunging to near-obscene depths. Making its appearance in the winter of 1923, the cloche hat (which became a symbol of the 1920s) completely covered the head from the eyebrows to the nape of the neck. Long hair, or hair pinned back in a bun, distorted the shape, however, which prompted women to cut their hair in the new, short styles. At the end of the decade, muffs were preferred over gloves to complement the now fashionable, fur-trimmed coats.

Left: Le Messager (The Messenger) *by Edouard Halouze features a dreamy woman in a low-cut, bejeweled gown. The lush background is pure Art Deco.*

Far left: A stencil by George Barbier from the almanac Guirlande des Mois, *1919.*

FASHION ACCESSORIES

Other popular Art Deco fashion accessories included fans, which ranged from the simple contemporary designs in paper (often featuring an advertisement on the reverse side) to delicate silk and satin fantasies on carved wooden frames. The mother-of-pearl fans of the Frenchman Georges Bastard were among the most lavish accessories of the time, their delicate ribs patterned with stylized flowers, triangles or other geometric shapes. Bastard also designed boxes, bowls, lanterns and a wide range of jewels – bangles, hat pins, haircombs – in mother of pearl, ivory, jade, tortoiseshell, horn, rock crystal and coral.

Handbags were usually quite small, either in a "clutch" style or with handles. They were sometimes covered with elaborate beading that was suspended from jewel-encrusted, silver, gold or platinum frames, or perhaps made of such exotic skins as lizard-, snake- or shark-skin (shagreen), and had gold or platinum clasps. Gemstones, accented with faceted or cabochon rubies, emeralds and sapphires and diamonds studded the frames. Semiprecious stones carved with Egyptian and Oriental-inspired motifs were used for the clasps.

HANDBAG MATERIALS

In the United States, steel mesh bags appeared, their metal frames frequently decorated with geometric designs in colorful enamels, or else studded with the cut-steel "jewels" known as marcasites (these were also popular diamond substitutes in cheap jewelry). Brocade, embroidered and tapestry bags were plentiful as well, adorned with jazzy, geometrical designs or colorful floral patterns. An evening bag designed by Van Cleef & Arpels was embroidered with sequins sewn onto the fabric. Mauboussin designed elaborate evening bags with diamond and emerald clasps that matched the brooches and bracelets worn on the bearer's evening gown. By the late 1930s plastic was emerging as a stylish material, and bulky handbags – often round or rectangular – began to be carried, sometimes even by women of taste.

The top designers of the day included Paul Poiret; Elsa Schiaparelli, who at times courted the ludicrous inventions of the Surrealist artists and, among her many classic costumes,

Above: A stylishly dressed couple poses on a paper fan, which would have been an advertising give-away.

Right: "The Polo Game," a fashion plate dating from 1923. The woman's accessories – her hat, gloves and parasol – reflect the Art Deco love of color.

wittily designed a hat topped by a shoe, and a gown shaped like a lobster; Coco Chanel; Jean Patou; Madeleine Vionnet (who invented the bias cut); Jeanne Lanvin; Worth; Nina Ricci; Paquin; Christian Berard; Lucien Lelong; Jacques Doucet; and Mainbocher. Coco Chanel revolutionized haute couture with her chic daytime designs, including the classic short and tailored two-piece suit.

ORPHIST FASHION

Some of the more jokey and humorous contributions to the Paris fashion scene were made by Sonia Delaunay, whose designs – like her brightly checked or zigzagged coats, dresses and hats – were influenced by the geometric elements of fine art. Her Orphist car was decorated in checks of bright color; the matching coats, hats and interior were impressive adaptations of her husband's serious high art.

They reflected the heady *joie de vivre* of the Art Deco style.

FASHION OUTSIDE FRANCE

Delaunay was quite serious about the whole enterprise: it was hard work creating fun; it was spirited, uplifting work. Her Orphist car, in particular, captured all the contradictions of Art Deco by means of one energetic leap into the machinery of the modern world. It was a remarkable feat of far-sightedness. Many of Delaunay's creations were quite similar to the avant-garde designs by the Russians Stepanova and Popova, with their practical lines and severe cuts quite removed from the heavily ornamented, exotic costumes of Poiret.

The contributions of other European countries and the United States were mostly pale reflections of what Paris was offering. Russia was deadly serious about the use of clothes

Above: "The Sweet Night" a fashion plate from the Gazette du Bon Ton, *1920, features clothes designed by Worth.*

Far left: Being geometric, the Greek key design on the frame of this French handbag fits nicely into Art Deco repertory.

Left: A detail of a smart clutch bag. The buckle is dotted with marcasites, which were popular imitation gems at the time.

design in relation to the ordinary people, as it was in ceramic design, but it was not any less inventive for that. Again, artists like Tatlin and Rodchenko applied themselves to the design of clothes fit for the average working Russian. The results were not elegant, but the stark frugality of the cut and material would have looked completely in place in any pavilion dedicated to *L'Esprit Nouveau*.

THE POPULARIZATION OF FASHION

Yet while the story of fashion during the 1920s and 1930s has often been represented as being exclusively that of the major couture houses located in Paris, the names of Schiaparelli, Paquin, Worth, Chanel and Balenciaga represent but one facet of what amounted to a growing obsession among the women and, to a lesser extent, the men of the world.

A UNIVERSAL STYLE

Far from being an upper-class domain, the new and stylish fashion was seen to percolate through every social rank in terms of clothing, hair and various accessories. Furthermore, the fashion of the upper – as well as of the middle and lower – classes was to a certain and unprecedented extent affected by the dress and appearance of the newly created, larger-than-life movie stars. For perhaps the first time, originality and novelty in fashion came from more than one source and what was fashionable and accepted as such could just as well originate from Hollywood – say, from the smart geometric haircut sported by Louise Brooks, or the sexy pajama suits of Marlene Dietrich – as from the French fashion journals. What is difficult to determine is where the impetus for actual change in fashion came from, and whether the stars of stage and screen were a reflection of, or a model for, popular taste.

The answer is that they were probably a combination of both, but what was immeasurably significant was the way in which style was disseminated to a huge audience.

In addition to movies, the growth of the women's magazine industry, particularly in the United States, provided an information outlet and a stimulation for demand. *Vogue, The Queen* and *Harper's Bazaar* all contributed to a fashion consciousness which, until the late 1920s at least, the ordinary woman had been aware of, but as something beyond her own sphere of experience. Now, for many more women than before, there existed the opportunity to be

Left: "The Seaside," a fashion plate from Art, Goût, Beauté, *1921, featuring designs by Molyneux, Beer, Doucet and Jenny.*

Below: Film stars like Joan Crawford influenced what ordinary women wore.

"fashionable" in a way which was truly a part of the swiftly changing modes and morals of the day. In short, the art of being fashionable was made easier by the fact that what was fashionable during the 1920s was so radically different from what had gone before.

The quest for contemporaneity could start with something as simple as a haircut: during the 1920s the bob, shingle, bingle or Eton crop. Hairstyles were always closely allied to other elements of prevailing fashion, and the reason for the shortness of the modern hairstyles during the 1920s may lie in the shift of the ever-changing focus on areas of the body as erogenous zones. Once again, the movies can be seen to play a role in this change in the public's taste. The vamp was born in silent American movies of the early 1920s, best realized by the likes of Pola Negri and Theda Bara. Because of the nature of acting for soundless movies, attention was focused on the eyes

Le Cadran Solaire

as tools of expression and dramatic effect. Kohl-rimmed orbs would glare in closeup from under exotic turbans or bandeaux pulled down over the brow, further accentuating the glowering, submissive, terrified or lustful stare of the ruby-red-lipped leading lady. It is no great leap to make between the look of the vamp smoldering under her turban, bandeau or close-fitting hat and the enormous popularity of the face-framing cloche hat which endured for most of the 1920s.

RISING HEMLINES

As we have seen, perhaps the most dramatic change in women's clothing was in the length of hemlines, which had been modestly low at the beginning of the 1920s but then shortened as the decade progressed. By 1925 the hemline had risen from the ankle to the knee, and once more the shifting erogenous zone was in evidence as the long-hidden female leg came boldly into view. What is more, it made its appearance clad in stockings, which were very often of flesh-colored silk or the newer, excitingly modern (and not to mention cheaper) rayon. This material was also used for underwear and evening dresses, and between 1920 and 1925 its production rose from 8 million lbs to 53 million lbs in the United States alone.

THE EMANCIPATED WOMAN

The shortening hemline can be allied, albeit tenuously, to the increasing emancipation of females, relating to both their consciousness and behavior. Newly fashionable dresses were related to the acceptance of jazz music in certain circles and the ability to move to the music was of paramount importance. The

Left: A fashion plate by George Barbier for the 1921 "Le Cadran Solaire."

reign of types of dress which were restrictive in this way therefore came swiftly to an end, for the young and fashionable realized that it was impossible to do the new dance called the "Charleston" in a hobble skirt or the "Black Bottom" in a whalebone corset.

THE CHANGING SILHOUETTE

Although the silhouette of the fashionable female was not subject to all of the rigors it had experienced in the previous century, body shape was still conditioned by the restrictive foundation garment called the "flattener." This was a device worn over the bust literally to flatten the profile of the woman, thus giving her a boyish physique commensurate with the fashionable boyish hairstyles. This in turn allowed for the "tube dress" to take precedence, a dress whose look paid no heed to the "ins and outs" of the female body. There was also the mass acceptance of the fashionable "jumper." First sold around 1922, the jumper was to form an integral part of the young woman's wardrobe. Generally, it was worn pulled down around the hips with a blouse underneath and a short pleated skirt. In terms of everyday fashion, this look was to endure to the end of the decade, and it is important, too, because it was a look transcending the boundaries of class.

BLURRING CLASS BOUNDARIES

The difference between mass fashion and couture, though, was realized through the types and qualities of materials used. The luxury of evening dresses and the social life that demanded them were, of course, the realm of high fashion and the rich, the glittering arena

Right: The front page of a 1920 issue of Le Rire *features a flapper versus a feminist.*

N° 96. — 4 Décembre 1920.
26ᵉ ANNÉE
France et Colonies   Étranger
Trois mois..... 9.50 10. »
Six mois..... 18. » 19.50
Un an....... 35. » 38. »
Les abonnements partent du 1ᵉʳ de chaque mois.

75 Centimes
F. JUVEN, éditeur
1, rue de Choiseul, 1
PARIS
Tout changement d'adresse doit être accompagné de 50 centimes.
Copyright 1920 by LE RIRE, Paris

Le Rire

JOURNAL HUMORISTIQUE PARAISSANT LE SAMEDI

TOTOTE EST CONSERVATRICE

— Moi, ma petite, je suis féministe.
— Eh bien ! pas moi : j'aime mieux les hommes.

Dessin de F. FABIANO.

29

in which the names of Chanel, Schiaparelli, Balenciaga and their other haute-couture contemporaries came into their own. For although some of their designs would eventually affect the contents of the ordinary working girl's wardrobe, their most immediate sphere of influence extended into the *beau monde*, of which they were a distinct part. Indeed, Schiaparelli was renowned for her concept of introducing styles inspired by honest working clothes into high society, once more shifting the impetus for change in clothing fashion.

THE STYLE OF THE 1930S

The beginning of the 1930s saw a turnaround by the leaders of fashion, who sought to lengthen the skirts which had reached their zenith of shortness at the peak of the jazz age. Perhaps it was the effects of the great slump, but the 1930s witnessed a dissolution of a single style for fashionable women and the embracing of many different styles, both in Europe and North America. Short hair and the cloche hat lost their supreme position and were replaced by longer, wavy locks and the small hat perched rakishly on the side of the head. This new style was accompanied by the lengthening of skirts until the hems were on average 10 in (25 cm) above the ground.

THE RETURN OF THE WAIST

The one concession to fashion which every woman was to make, regardless of the style or detailing of the rest of her dress, was in the waist. The return of the boned corset was only interrupted by the demands on both bodies and materials occasioned by the outbreak of World War II. The small waist was, more often than not, complemented by an exaggeration in the width of the shoulders, a look in part prompted by Joan Crawford.

Above: This fashion plate appeared in Art, Goût, Beauté *in 1921. The slim line of the dress, its high neck and the elaborate, plumed hat were common features of the haute couture of the 1920s.*

In the realms of haute couture and evening wear the area of emphasis shifted once again and the back came into its own. Indeed, even some day wear was slit at the back to show bare skin. This trend grew along with the general public passion for sport and sportswomen, which was especially strong during the 1930s. In swimming and tennis, for instance, the clothes worn by both the professionals and amateurs became much more practical and, because of this, much more revealing. The growth of golf as a game for both men and women also meant that fashionable ladies were seen attired in practical and clothing on the links. The growth of sunbathing and the belief in the beneficial effects of a suntan – as well as its social cachet – also meant that flesh had to be revealed rather than concealed.

Above: The actress Marlene Dietrich dressed in the height of fashion.

Left: This stained-glass window by Jacques Gruber reflects the golfing craze.

MEN'S FASHIONS

In terms of men's clothing, cut had resolved itself by the mid-1920s and the greatest changes to occur were in the choice of materials. The suit continued to be a staple of the average man's wardrobe, but there was a distinct and growing move toward the casual, which continued through the 1920s and into the 1930s. Notwithstanding the elegance of the upper-class male in top hat and tails, personified by Fred Astaire, the everyday man was seen in the suit, which changed only in small details. By the mid-1920s, the vest had fallen out of favor, prompting the move to the double-breasted coat. By the end of the decade, however, the vest was back in fashion, worn as a double-breasted garment under a single-breasted coat.

MEN'S PANTS

By far the most outrageous change in the cut of men's clothing between the wars was in the width of the pants. The "Oxford Bag," so called because the style was originated and adopted by the undergraduates of Oxford University, gained rapid popularity, but this had diminished by the end of the 1920s. Yet the width of the pant leg was still to remain relatively wide until the end of the 1930s. Other men's-wear novelties included plus fours (short trousers for shooting which were adopted for golfing and then for town wear), the motoring cap, the boater and the blazer. All these were peripheral developments however, and were set against the changing backdrop of social and economic upheaval which characterized these fashion-fixated years.

Below left: A jaunty caricature of the French performer Maurice Chevalier, sporting a straw boater and suntan.

Below: A pencil and gouache fashion illustration by Ernest Deutsch Dryden.

Art Deco
Jewelry & Fashion
Accessories

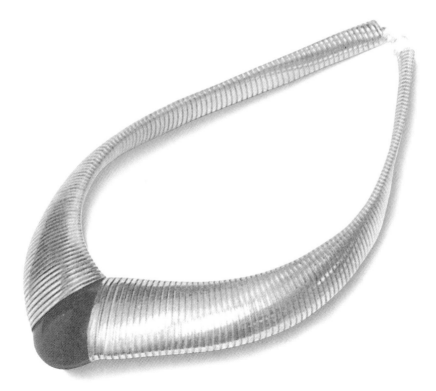

Jewelry is often regarded as a trivial luxury, a little extra touch that sets off an article of clothing. Apart from the wonderful creations by Jean Puiforcat in the area of tableware, it is in the field of jewelry that Art Deco reaches the zenith of its stylishness. If the designs for furniture or building interiors sometimes looked clumsy or not quite right, the intimate scale of jewelry could disguise those shortcomings. Indeed, jewelry is one of the most exciting disciplines of the 1920–30 era.

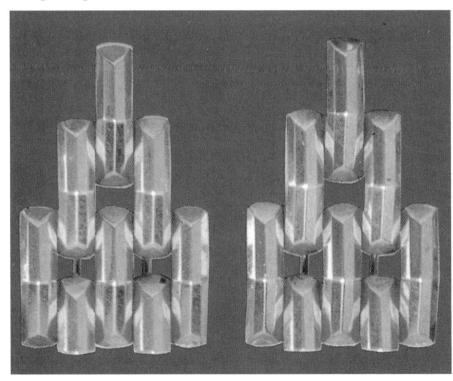

Preceding page: This chrome necklace is strikingly set off by pieces of bright synthetic plastic. The chain is intricately fashioned, solid yet flexible, and easily worn.

Above: The outstanding manifestation of Art Deco in the United States was its architecture. Some architectonic jewelry was inspired by skyscrapers, and these stepped gold clips are by Tiffany & Co.

The jewelers of the Art Deco period produced some of the most dazzling pieces ever seen – daring, pristine and even playful. Unlike the Art Nouveau and Arts and Crafts periods, when noted designers held prime positions and had a strong influence on other individuals, the Art Deco years were strong on design itself; many quintessential pieces were anonymously designed, unsigned (except perhaps for a jeweler's mark), and indeed of uncertain national origin. So wide-ranging and pervasive a style was Art Deco that similar pieces – necklaces of, say, Bakelite and chrome – were being manufactured in places as disparate as New Jersey and Czechoslovakia.

THE GEOMETRIC INFLUENCE

While the Art Nouveau movement freed jewelry design from the antiquated influences of the nineteenth century, Art Deco took this evolution a step farther, introducing geometrical forms and brilliant color schemes. Unlike Art Nouveau jewelry, which often involved realistic floral, figural or faunal motifs, Art Deco was simpler; it was usually either geometric or abstract, and even when it featured flowers or other realistic elements these were quite subtle and underplayed.

FREEDOM OF EXPRESSION

The jewelry and accessories of the Art Deco period were as varied and colorful as the fashions themselves. The great French goldsmiths created miniature works of art in platinum, gold, diamonds, emeralds and other precious gems – some starkly geometric, others with Egyptian or Oriental overtones, still others wildly floral and encrusted with stones of many colors. Such hard stones as onyx, turquoise, jade and lapis lazuli were also used, and enameling was widely applied.

The myriad influences contributing to Art Deco jewelry came from pharoanic Egypt, the Orient, tribal Africa, from machines and graphic design, even from buildings, such as stepped Mayan temples and their latter-day descendants, the big-city skyscrapers. The abstract qualities of Art Deco jewelry can be traced to some of various avant-garde art movements that arose during the first decade of the twentieth century.

THE INFLUENCE OF ART

Picasso's *Demoiselles d'Avignon,* painted in 1907, launched the Cubist movement in its division of the human figure into flat, overlapping, geometric configurations. In 1909 the Italian poet Marinetti published the *Futurist Manifesto,* which heralded the machine, urban life and speed as the pictorial expression of a new reality. The Dutch De Stijl painter Piet Mondrian took Cubism a step farther, into neoplasticism. Through abstraction, he freed forms from any suggestion of objective reality.

As early as 1913, many of these new artistic concepts were evident in jewelry design, particularly in France. In the United States, where modernism in jewelry design was resisted fiercely for many years, a critic for the *Jewelers' Circular Weekly* (of March 26, 1913) asked, "Will the new movement in painting and sculpture be reflected in the forthcoming jewelry?" The article went on to conclude, concerning Cubism and Futurism, that "whether the exhibits appeal to us or not the vital impulse toward something new and simple is apparent on every hand."

ART DECO MOTIFS

The principle motifs in Art Deco jewelry design were simple geometric forms, such as the square, circle, rectangle and triangle. These

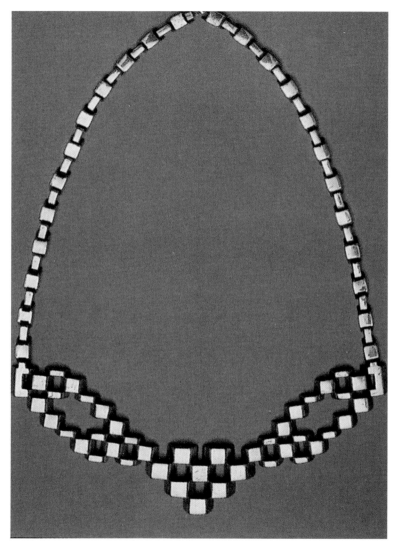

Above: An intricately fashioned essay in geometry, this 1930s' gilded-metal necklace has a strong machine-age feel. The piece is French, but its maker is unknown.

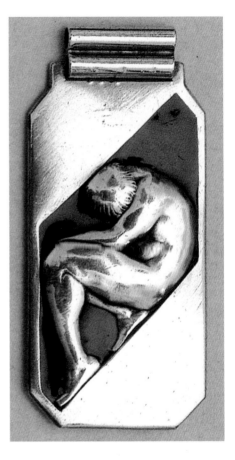

Above: An Arcadian pipe-player occupies a roundel of pavé-set diamonds in this brooch by Boucheron dating from c.1910.

Right: A handsome enameled-silver pendant made by French jeweler Emile Davide during the 1920s.

shapes were often juxtaposed or overlapped to create complex linear configurations. Abstract patterns, derived from the architecture of ancient civilizations, such as Babylonian ziggurats and stepped Mayan and Aztec temples, also found their way into the contours of jewelry design. Although images of animals of speed and grace – the greyhound, the gazelle and the deer – as well as of the new-fangled automobiles and airplanes were found on both precious and mass-produced jewels,

human subjects were not as common as on Art Nouveau goldsmiths' work, but some noted designers depicted them in their creations, and, more often, they appeared on inexpensive, anonymous baubles.

CLASSICAL INSPIRATION

René Lalique molded some of his pendants on romantic women; stylized African heads formed brooches by Chanel and others; Emile Davide favored the handsome, neo-classical

figure; and stylish 1920s' women were cut from cheap white metals, sometimes attached by tiny chains to modish canines.

Sir Flinders Petrie's archeological excavations during the first decade of the century started an Egyptian craze. Howard Carter's discovery of Tutankhamen's tomb in 1922, and the press coverage that this generated for ten years, ensured a continuing interest in Egyptian art. The clean lines of hieroglyphic calligraphy reiterated the linear concepts that had begun to emerge before the war. Van Cleef & Arpels, among others, introduced stylized pharoanic motifs into their series of bracelets, shoulder clips and brooches. Diamonds, rubies, emeralds and sapphires were interchanged with such neutral stones as onyx.

GEMS AND METALS

The materials used by the Art Deco jewelry-makers ranged from the traditional and precious to the unorthodox and innovative, like plastic, chrome and steel. Art Deco jewelry incorporated gold and silver, and precious and semiprecious stones, in designs that emphasized their contrasting colorative effects. Strong, earthy and unrefined colors dominated. Semiprecious stones, such as amber, jade, lapis lazuli, coral, turquoise, topaz, tourmaline, onyx, amethyst, aquamarine and rock crystal (some of which had been incorporated into Art Nouveau jewelry) gave jewelry settings vibrancy and interest, especially when placed next to such precious stones as diamonds (mostly baguette cut) and emeralds. Faceted and flat stones provided additional contrast in their different surface treatments.

As with furniture, the use of exotic new stones and metals was promoted. No longer limited to the traditional precious stones and metals, the jewelry designers made full use of new materials. Until 1900, stones were set almost exclusively in gold and sterling silver, often to the visual detriment of a piece of jewelry. The discovery of platinum as a setting in the first decade of the twentieth century, and its perfection a few years later – it was used in the manufacture of explosives during World War I – and adoption as a setting meant that the other elements could be accentuated. Platinum is a far stronger metal than gold or silver, which allows a stone to be set with very little supporting mounting. The settings for stones could therefore be reduced to just two or three retaining teeth. Art Deco jewelry therefore became both lighter in weight and more delicate in appearance. Van Cleef & Arpels developed the *serti invisible* (invisible setting), in which several rows of stones are placed next to each other with no apparent mounting. Although this technique was not perfected until 1935, a few pieces of the firm's jewelry from the early 1920s have survived to show its initial experiments.

MODERN MATERIALS

Other new materials used were onyx, ebony, chrome, plastic, lapis lazuli, lacquered metals, agate, coral, Bakelite, rhinestones, jade, tortoiseshell, jet and moonstone. Used in conjunction, these materials offered up a riot of color and contrasting textures. The types of jewelry and also accessories produced were

Below: This diamond, ruby, emerald and sapphire bracelet by Lacloche Frères exemplifies the Egyptian-revival aspect of Art Deco.

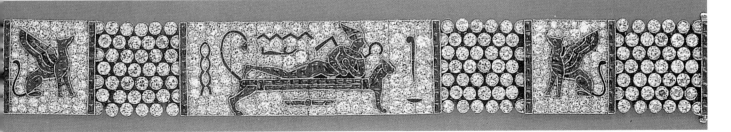

as varied as the materials available: cigarette holders, rings, geometric necklaces, diamond and jet pins, glass pendants and wristwatches for day and evening wear. It was the pearl, however, that became a dominant gem of the period. During the nineteenth century, Oriental pearls had been treasured because of their scarcity. George Gould, son of the railway magnate Jay Gould, is reputed to have spent $500,000 on a string of pearls as a gift for his wife. After Mikimoto developed a technique for producing cultured pearls in Japan, however, pearls were available to a wider market. They could be set with other stones, worn in chokers around the neck, or in single strands, and became the accepted accessories for any occasion. A testimony to the popularity of pearls during the 1920s is evidenced by the following quotation from *Vogue* magazine: "Day after day, I used to see poor Regina frying in that Lido in torture getting her neck brown. She did it, of course, for her pearls."

By 1929 the jeweler's more abstract creations had evolved into mechanistic forms based on industrial design. Indeed, the modern design principles inherent in automobile and airplane construction inspired a new decorative vocabulary for jewelry. Jewelry design had evolved from the thin, delicate creations of the early 1920s into bolder, larger designs with sharp outlines. The rainbow palette of bright colors gave way to muted tones. Stark contrast was achieved with black and white, epitomized by onyx and diamonds. Indeed, the diamond reigned supreme, cut in the new baguette style and placed next to other stones for contrast. There was also a return to the colored diamond.

Left: A white-gold brooch, probably French, set with emeralds, rubies, diamonds and moonstones.

Below: A silver, malachite and sodalite brooch made in the 1930s by Jean Desprès.

FASHION'S INFLUENCE
Although many of the changes that took place

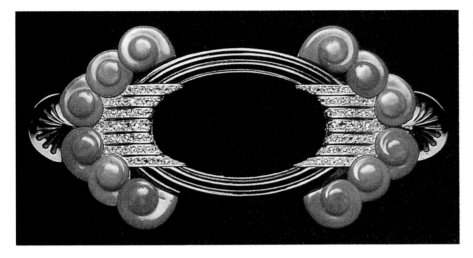

Left: Charles Massé designed this platinum, coral, onyx, and diamond brooch for Boucheron in 1925.

Below: A pair of emerald and diamond earrings by Van Cleef & Arpels.

in the field of jewelry design during the 1920s and 1930s occurred primarily for artistic reasons, fashion also directly influenced the style, size and shape of Art Deco jewelry. The introduction of rayon and muslin – materials too light to bear the weight of a heavy piece of jewelry – necessitated lighter pieces, now made possible with platinum. The new style in women's clothing – cloche hats, short hair, short hemlines, short sleeves – had furthermore changed the type of jewelry that was required to set the look off, and it demanded complementary forms and types. The new look necessitated new jewelry with simple lines, minimum design and vivid colors.

NECKLACES

Sleeveless, low-cut dresses accentuated the two main areas where jewels could be worn: the neck and the wrists. In order to accentuate the vertical line of the tubular dress, jewelry designers introduced long, dangling necklaces influenced by the multistranded models of the Indian maharajahs. Women wore such *sautoirs*

and strings of beads in materials such as ivory, wood and semiprecious stones, either in the traditional manner or hanging down the back, over one shoulder, or even wrapped round one leg. Necklaces, suspended with pendants and tassels, hung as far as the stomach or, on occasion, even to the knees. In the dance-crazy "Roaring Twenties," long necklaces complemented the short tunic dresses, fast dances and swaying movements.

BROOCHES

The simple dresses, in contrast to the turn-of-the-century styles, and the simple hats could be decorated with small brooches (pins) and clasps. Brooches were worn attached to hats, shoulders, straps or belts. Perhaps the most important single innovation was the invention of the double-sided clip or clasp. The clips could be used in pairs to hold material together, or separately as brooches and pins. Such versatile, multiple-use jewelry (that is, pieces comprising two or more components which could be dismantled and used separately) became

Right: Georges Fouquet fashioned this gold brooch. Many of his pieces displayed a machine-age sensibility

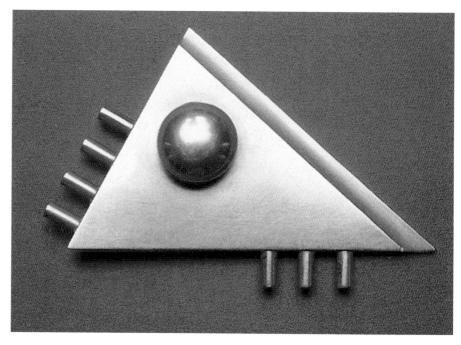

popular after the crash of 1929 and during the subsequent Depression. Pendants could double as brooches or be attached to lapels. The double barrette, formed from two linked pins, could be separated and worn in two places. The finest pieces came from the major jewelry houses, but they were also imitated in less expensive materials for the mass market.

BROOCH-BUCKLES

At the cheaper end of the scale, hundreds of different designs were brought out for buttons used on everyday wear. The brooch-buckle was composed of a ring of onyx, crystal or coral, either in a circle or an ellipse, with decorative motifs at either end using diamonds, pearls or sapphires. Black, Starr & Frost advertised a typical example in 1926 set with oxblood coral, diamonds and onyx. The brooch-buckle and the pin – another piece of jewelry which became popular during this period – could be worn either on a belt or else attached to the cloche, the hat which sat securely on the wearers' heads over their fashionably cropped, shingled or bobbed hair.

EARRINGS AND BANDEAUX

Such short hairstyles not only did away with the demand for elaborate extras like combs, but also exposed the ear for the first time, and long, dangling earrings of diamond, jade, ivory, jet, onyx, crystal and amber became fashionable, while small ear clips also appeared in myriad handsome guises. By 1929 earrings were so long that they touched the shoulder, further emphasizing the verticality of fashion.

In response to the new, slender fashions at the beginning of the century, the bandeau had replaced the tiara and diadem. Still desired as an ornament worn in the evening, women in the 1920s wore the bandeau on the hairline, or set back on the head, like a halo.

In 1930 the French jeweler Chaumet designed an elegant diamond bandeau with three rosettes and stylized foliage. While, in the United States, Oscar Heyman & Bros., a jeweler's jeweler which still manufactures fine jewelry for other prestigious firms, designed a delicate, diamond-studded example.

Because the typical Art Deco dress was sleeveless, it allowed the jewelry designer free rein to design creative jewelry with which to decorate the wrists and upper arm. There were several types of bracelets. The first were flat,

Above: A red and black piece of jewelry by Boucheron, c.1925.

Left: A simple rock-crystal, platinum and diamond pendant necklace created by Georges Fouquet in 1924.

Above: A pair of jade, onyx and diamond earrings fashioned by Boucheron of Paris.

Above right: A diamond, aquamarine and giant-citrine pendant brooch made by the Parisian firm Maison Mellerrio.

flexible, narrow bands decorated with stylized designs of flowers, geometricized shapes and motifs from Egypt and Persia. Because these were narrow, four or five were worn together on the wrist. Toward the end of the 1920s they became wider. Big, square links of coral, rock crystal, onyx, and *pavé* diamonds were accentuated with emeralds, rubies, sapphires, and other cabochon-cut gems. Other types, bangles or slave bracelets, were worn on the upper arm or just above the elbow. They were made out of gold, silver and materials such as bamboo. Like the flexible bracelets, several were worn at a time.

EVENING BRACELETS

Artist-jewelers like Jean Fouquet, Raymond Templier, Jean Desprès, and Gérard Sandoz combined a variety of stones and metals. In Sweden, Wiwen Nilsson mixed silver with large pieces of crystal. A third type, worn in the evening, consisted of loose strands of pearls held together by a large, pearl-studded medallion from which additional strings of pearls were suspended. Like the bangle, it was worn above the elbow. A vogue that was to have little effect on the top-class jewelers was the wearing of heavy, primitive bangles, although Jean Fouquet was one of the few to exploit the fashion with African-style bracelets.

With sleeveless dresses and the rage for sports, the watch bracelet became very popular during the 1920s. Jean Patou introduced the *garçonne*-type (the boyish woman) into fashion when he outfitted the tennis star Suzanne Lenglen. Every woman wanted to look the part of the sportswoman, even if she did not participate.

WRISTWATCHES

Cartier is credited with designing the world's first wristwatch, as well as what some consider the most significant wristwatch ever made: the "Tank" watch. The wristwatch, worn during the day, was plain and strapped with leather or ribbon. The evening watch resembled a richly jeweled bracelet set with pearls and diamonds, either enameled or made of different colors of gold. An example from the period by Tiffany & Co. was set with diamonds and onyx and mounted in platinum. Between 1925 and 1930 the pendant and châteleine watches became popular. Suspended from a

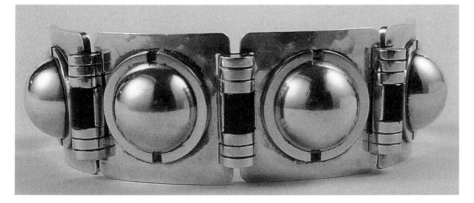

Left: This gilt-silver and onyx articulated bracelet is by Jean Desprès, 1930.

Below: A 1930s' multilinked bracelet made of enameled and silvered white metal.

Below: The firm of Louis Cartier fashioned this pendant watch of diamonds, jade, onyx and sapphires (shown front and back).

ribbon or silk cord, the face of the watch was upside down so that the wearer could glance downward to determine the time. (An example by Van Cleef & Arpels shows its Eastern influence with its jade, enameling and Oriental motifs; this pendant watch, suspended from a *sautoir* chain, was worn in the evening. The chain was studded with pearls, diamonds and coloured gems. Its case was also embellished with diamonds.)

After World War I, rings grew far larger and bolder, dominating the finger. Surfaces were smooth, polished or satinized metals. Stones could be either precious or semiprecious, set with *pavé* diamonds or a combination of two lacquered metals.

Toward the end of the 1920s, when gloves went out of fashion and muffs were preferred for the new, fur-trimmed coats, women began to wear massive rings to adorn their now

Above: A cocktail watch by Paul-Emile Brandt, its platinum bracelet highlighted with diamonds and emeralds.

Far left and left: Three tiny rhinestone and paste timepieces, with Swiss-made works and elaborate frames. They could be worn as brooches or pendants.

gloveless hands. The popularity of the fan as an accessory for evening wear gave them a further opportunity to show off the latest in ring fashions. Suzanne Belperron's large ring in carved chalcedony, set with a single Oriental pearl, captured the new mood.

VARIED INSPIRATIONS

Other ring designers offered widely different solutions. Jean Desprès combined crystal, gold and silver to make abstract geometric patterns influenced by Cubism and African masks; Fritz Schwerdt, working in Germany, designed rings that were inspired by machines, one of which reproduced precisely the inner mechanism of a rotary engine in which an agate rod acted as the connecting pin.

MEN'S JEWELRY

The Art Deco style was also reflected in men's jewelry, although never with the same flair as women's. Geometric forms characterized the dials of men's pocket watches, which were mounted in platinum set with onyx, diamonds,

pearls, emeralds, rubies, and topazes. Watch chains were made up of cylinder links enhanced with polished or faceted stones. Cufflinks followed the same general shapes. Jean Fouquet designed a notable pair with enameled Cubist motifs; Black, Starr & Frost's selection included a pair made of onyx with diamond borders.

BEJEWELED FASHION ACCESSORIES

Fashion accessories – vanity cases, handbags, powder compacts, fans, cigarette cases – were designed in abundance during the 1920s and 1930s, often with bold geometric and floral motifs that were every bit as masterful as those decorating furniture, ceramics and textiles. Mauboussin, Lacloche Frères, Fouquet, Marchak, Mellerio, Tiffany & Co., Boucheron, Cartier, Chaumet, and Van Cleef & Arpels were some of the major jewelers whose output included not only standard jewelry items but also fashion accessories for the well-dressed lady of the period and an amazing variety of *objets d'art*, some of which are really more jewelry than object, with elements carved in semiprecious stones set in silver and gold and often elaborately lacquered. Influenced by Chinese, Japanese, Persian and medieval art, these *objets d'art* combined colored gemstones, precious stones, marcasite, enamel and lacquer. The small cigarette cases designed by Gérard Sandoz introduced a further type of decoration in their use of crushed *coquille d'oeuf* (eggshell). Whether it was a vanity or cigarette case, compact, lighter, lipstick case, mirror or handbag, each item was intended as a miniature work of art.

Left: Casino de Paris performer Mistinguett flaunts her elaborate ring and bracelets in this poster by Charles Gesmar, 1925.

Left: Van Cleef & Arpel's elaborate vanity case features a Japanese landscape of inlaid gold, abalone and mother of pearl.

Below left: This Van Cleef & Arpels vanity case is primarily of lapis lazuli, with a carved center panel dotted with diamonds.

CARTIER'S *OBJETS D'ART*

By 1920, for example, Cartier's *oeuvre* included such luxury *objets* as vanity cases, jewel caskets, lighters and timepieces. Cartier's pieces were highly decorative, and often pictorial. He created vanity cases adorned with Chinese landscapes in mother of pearl, colored enamels and rubies. The *nécessaire*, or vanity case, which held a mirror, compact, lipstick and comb, took its form from the Japanese *inro* (a small case divided into several compartments). Although small in size, it accommodated all of the accouterments that a lady might need.

NEW FORMS OF ACCESSORIES

Vanities were mostly rectangular or oval, and hung from a silk cord. In 1930 the vanity case was enlarged into the *minaudière* by Alfred Van Cleef, who named it this after witnessing his wife simper (*minauder*) into the mirror. The *minaudière* replaced the evening bag and daytime dress bag.

Powder compacts and cigarette cases became *de rigueur* during the 1920s for the bold woman of fashion, who could now smoke and powder her nose in public. Inexpensive versions of these items, as well as of vanity cases, also proliferated, especially in France and the United States. These were fashioned of paste, plastic, and base metal, and the application of colored enamel to the metal pieces often made them – despite being cheap and mass-produced – every bit as

handsome as the more expensive models. They were sometimes marked with the cosmetic firm's name – Richard Hudnut, Coty, Helena Rubenstein – but were more often engraved with such evocative words as Volupté or Zanadu. One Coty compact was covered all over with a René Lalique design of stylized powder puffs in black, orange, white and gold; the same design appeared on a cardboard powder box and has recently been in production again.

THE USE OF INDUSTRIAL METAL

Firms who manufactured industrial metal, such as Elgin American in Illinois, diversified to produce compacts and vanity cases which were often superbly engineered in enameled chrome or another white metal and which sold for a dollar or less. Many of the cheaper varieties of accessories sported either figural or faunal decorative designs – stylishly clad ladies, graceful deer or greyhounds, playful Scotties, for example. Enameled cigarette cases for both men and women were covered with rich geometric, sunburst or zigzag patterns, or were often adorned with a stone stud or two.

Above left: A black enamel compact set with diamonds by Cartier, c.1925.

Above: This compact and matching lipstick case by Elgin American is handsomely presented as a boxed set.

NOTED
ART DECO
JEWELERS

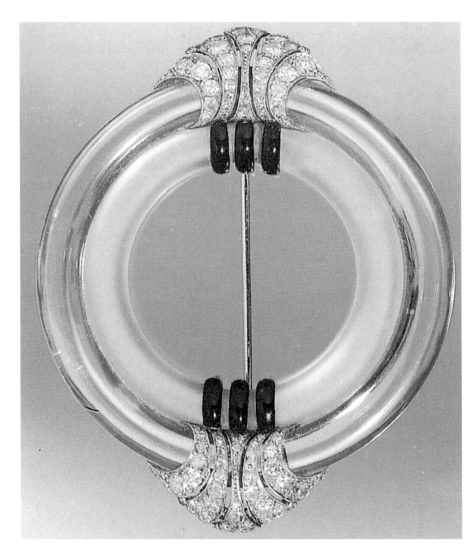

The Swiss-born designer Jean Dunand, whose hammered-metal and lacquered vases, furniture and screens were greatly indebted to Asian and other non-Western styles, also designed a small but stunning body of jewelry. Largely of hammered silver lacquered with red and black, Dunand's dangling earrings and earclips, brooches and bracelets, came to assume bold geometric shapes containing equally strong motifs – interwoven or superimposed lines, zigzags, openwork squares and triangles, and so on. Their kinship with the painting of the time is immediately evident, and indeed Dunand often collaborated with Cubist painter and sculptor Jean Lambert-Ruckion on large projects. He produced a particularly striking pair of earrings with dangling black enamel grids which were reminiscent in style of the *"Gitterwerk"* of turn-of-the-century Vienna.

FOUQUET PÈRE ET FILS

Georges and Jean Fouquet were father and son and both created outstanding jewels during the Art Deco period. Georges, who had also produced Art Nouveau goldsmith's work for La Maison Fouquet, tended toward busier designs, whereas Jean leaned to more geometric forms, *à la* Templier and Sandoz "art jewels." The firm also commissioned jewelry from Eric Bagge, the noted architect and interior designer; painter André Leveille; and the premier poster artist-illustrator of the day, A. M. Cassandre.

Paris, of course, was both the source and the trendsetter of Art Deco, so it follows that it should have led the way in *moderne* jewelry, and many renowned French goldsmiths created lovely, often one-of-a-kind, jewels for their exclusive clientele.

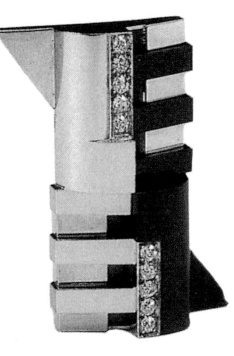

GÉRARD SANDOZ

Gérard Sandoz came from a noted family of jewelry-makers, and began to design stark, geometric pieces for the Sandoz firm while still in his teens. His goldsmith's *oeuvre* dates from a period of just under a decade, yet his output is nonetheless significant within the realm of Art Deco jewelry. The clean lines and delicate craftsmanship of Sandoz's undeniably machine-age pieces, with smooth, shiny or matt metal "parts" featuring materials like onyx and coral, and punctuated by a single aquamarine "stud" or a line of diamonds, contributed to their significant place in the Art Deco repertoire. This work spanned only about a decade, for he later turned to movie-making and painting.

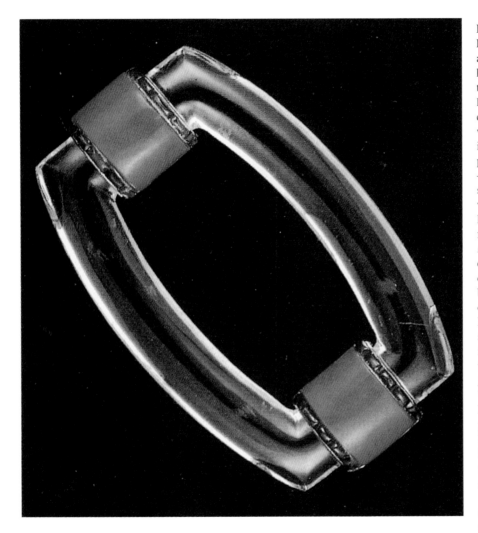

Above: This rock crystal, coral, onyx, and sapphire brooch by the Parisian firm of René Boivin is a lovely example of a sparsely geometric, subtly colored jewel.

RAYMOND TEMPLIER

Raymond Templier, like Sandoz, came from a family of Parisian jewelers, Maison Templier having been started by his grandfather during the mid-nineteenth century. Templier's designs, like Deprès's, were boldly geometric, but sported more precious stones, for instance brooches with scatterings of diamonds against stark platinum fields. Templier was especially fond of precious white metals – platinum and silver – and paired them with onyx and other dark stones in stunning pieces (these black-and-white color combinations were wildly popular during the Art Deco period). His designs for the actress Brigitte Helm's jewels in the movie *L'Argent* were marvelously theatrical, especially in the blatantly architectonic ear pendants which could be miniature Empire State buildings or John Storrs sculptures. Templier collaborated with the designer Michel Percheron and at least once with the Cubist sculptor-painter Gustave Miklos, whose delicate plaster model of an elongated head he translated into a brooch of white and yellow gold. A bracelet containing a brooch in the Virginia Museum of Fine Art's collection in Richmond, Virginia, is an outstanding example of his intricate designs: the wide, silver band centers on a removable brooch of platinum, white gold and diamonds, which is itself rectilinear but which features a large, round diamond.

Other noted Art Deco "art jewelers," whose output was small but significant in terms of design, included Paul-Emile Brandt and René Boivin, whose firm produced its handsome *moderne* designs under the direction of Madame Boivin and her two daughters. Much more prolific, however, and in turn influential, were the mostly long-established jewelry firms producing *deluxe* pieces – Cartier,

Boucheron, Janesich, Chaumet, Mellerio, Fouquet, Vever, and Van Cleef & Arpels.

LOUIS CARTIER

The Cartier firm produced more traditional and less geometric jewels. Louis Cartier (1875–1942) was the third generation of his family to head the House of Cartier in Paris, which had been founded by his grandfather in 1847. Cartier was fascinated by the Ballets Russes, and was also influenced by the arts of Egypt, the Islamic world, and the Orient, as well as by the craftsmanship of the legendary Peter Carl Fabergé, goldsmith to the Russian imperial family.

ORIENTAL INFLUENCES

The year 1910 was a significant one for Cartier: upon viewing the Ballets Russes's production of *Scheherezade*, he and his assistant Charles Jacqueau altered not only the firm's palette but also the types of gems they used. The colors and designs of Cartier's jewels now became quite daring and innovative, as did the actual composition of the pieces, which featured both precious and semiprecious gems in dramatic settings. Geometric patterns appeared, but when compared with the bold, stark designs of Templier, Sandoz and others, Cartier's jewels were extremely decorative, even pictorial: his diamond brooches, for example, taking the form of overflowing flower baskets, while also common to his repertory were elaborate figural motifs inspired by the exotic worlds of India, Egypt, and the Middle and Far East.

Right: A stunning cigarette case by Cartier, worked in mother of pearl, coral, and diamonds. Note especially the turtle with its red shell.

Above: A diamond and platinum cornucopia brooch by an unknown French maker.

Right: A winged scarab brooch by Cartier, 1924. The body is of smoked quartz, the wings of faience and emeralds.

EXOTIC INSPIRATION

Cartier's fascination with exotic motifs led to the creation of diamond, ruby, and platinum earrings from which hung jade roundels carved with elephants, and a gold and enamel bangle with two carved-stone chimera heads facing each other in the center.

FIGURAL MOTIFS

During the 1930s, figural clips and brooches, featuring ornate "blackamoor" heads, and even Native American squaws and chiefs, were marketed by Cartier and spawned a whole wave of cheap imitations, especially in plastics and base metals. A great deal of carved jade and coral was used in Cartier's rings, brooches, jabot pins, bracelets, and necklaces, and motifs such as heavily bejeweled baskets or swags of flowers, berries, and fruit (popularly known as either "fruit salads" or "tutti frutti") were composed of rich, colorful masses of carved emeralds, rubies and sapphires amid variously cut and set diamonds. Jewelers also engraved emeralds, jade, coral, and lapis lazuli in imitation of Oriental jewelry (the stones were often carved in the Orient and shipped to the West for setting).

THE CHANGING STYLE

Cartier, Black, Starr & Frost, J. E. Caldwell & Co., and Van Cleef & Arpels mixed engraved stones in figurative compositions, such as animals and baskets of fruit and flowers, that took their inspiration from Japanese and Egyptian prototypes. Such motifs worked their way into the ever-growing repertoire of costume jewelry too, with French, American, Czechoslovakian, and other factories flooding the market with paste resembling diamonds, rubies, emeralds, onyx and jade. By the end of the 1920s, jewelers refined gem-

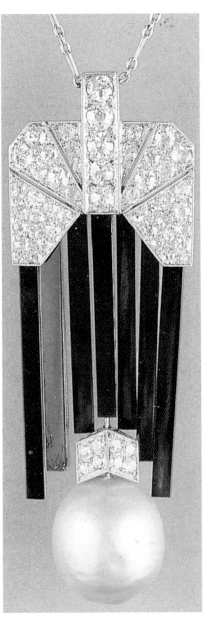

Left: A pendant by Lacloche Frères fashioned from platinum, diamonds, onyx, and pearl.

Below: A pendant shaped in the form of a pagoda by the German firm Theodor Fahrner.

cutting further by the introduction of several new shapes, such as the baguette, trapezium, table, and square cut.

GLASS JEWELRY

The glass jewelry of René Lalique – the undisputed *maître verrier* (master of glass) – and Gabriel Argy-Rousseau deserves special mention. By the 1920s Lalique was creating some spectacular glass jewelry, including round and oval medallions molded with female figures, insects and flowers, some in bright hues, others in subtly stained frosted glass. He also created all-glass rings, molded with tiny flowers; expandable bracelets of wide rectangular sections decorated with stylized organic designs; necklaces made up partly or wholly of hemispherical, zigzag, floral, foliate or round beads; and brooches and buckles backed by colored foil and metal depicting subjects as varied as moths, a satyr, serpents, and a grazing stag. His pendants, some inspired by openwork Japanese swordguards, or *tsubas*, and molded with stylized leaf or animal designs, others with insects and beautiful female figures, all hung from silk cords terminating in rich tassels.

GABRIEL ARGY-ROUSSEAU

Pâte-de-verre master Argy-Rousseau also produced jewelry: one of his diamond-shaped pendants features a white elephant in a leafy surround; a round medallion depicts a curtsying ballerina amid a floral border; and a further pendant – this one oval – has three scarab beetles, one of many Egyptian motifs made popular during the 1920s.

Left: Sybil Dunlop created this long 1930s' necklace, with a tassel pendant and matching clips of silver and chrysoprase.

Among the other well-known *deluxe* designers, Mauboussin was noted for his highly colorful pieces, often set in black enamel; Boucheron continued to make great use of the diamonds which had made the firm famous during the late nineteenth century, only now they were literally combined with lapis lazuli, jade, coral, onyx, and other semiprecious stones; while the jewels of Lacloche Frères, Chaumet, Linzeler & Marshak, Dusausoy, and so many other firms sparkled their way into the jewelry boxes and onto the necks, arms, and clothes of the fashionable and rich men and women of the 1920s.

Elsewhere, the style was neither widespread nor much imitated, although occasional pieces were produced in Italy, Germany, and Britain during the late 1920s. The Italian G. Ravasco's diamond-studded geometric creations, or German jeweler Theodor Fahrner's later jewels, for example, were largely derivative of the noted French jewelers' designs, while Switzerland's expert watchmakers, many of whose designers were in any case often French, created cases with subtle geometric motifs.

BRITISH JEWELERS

Some London jewelers, like Asprey and Mappin & Webb, produced Art Deco-style confections, but these are largely unsigned, so the designers are unknown.

Some British designers, however, like Sybil Dunlop, Harold Stabler and H. G. Murphy, known primarily for their Arts and Crafts-style pieces, produced decidedly *moderne* (though not geometric) jewels. The Copenhagen firm of Georg Jensen, the Danish silversmith, produced silver jewelry in the Art Deco era (and some gold as well), adding sharp geometric forms to its repertoire of stylized motifs. Animal subjects – especially the perennially popular deer – as well as flowers and leaves, adorned brooches, bracelets, and buckles, and these in turn were imitated by a host of European and American jewelers.

AMERICAN JEWELRY

American jewelry in the Art Deco period was

mostly designed in the French style by such fine firms as Tiffany & Co., Udall & Ballou, Spaulding-Gorham, and C. D. Peacock. Bracelets, brooches, and pendants were sometimes starkly geometric, but were far more often either simple floral arrangements or dazzling masses of colored gems and diamonds. These included Oriental-inspired pieces, like a bracelet from Marsh & Co. (a San Francisco jeweler), its carved coral plaques alternating with iron sections enclosing Chinese characters; architectonic confections, like a pair of gold Tiffany clips comprising stepped sections of tiny squares; and Egyptian-revival baubles, such as Marcus & Co.'s opal brooch with an elaborate gold setting featuring a pharaoh and his queen, a scarab beetle, and lotus flowers.

THE AMERICAN STYLE

The indigenous Mexican silver industry was highlighted in the Art Deco era as a result of the talents of American architect-designer-teacher William Spratling, who settled in Taxco in 1929. He opened a store dealing in traditional crafts and also started a school where he trained native people to work with silver and other local substances. Spratling produced some stunning brooches, bracelets, and earrings, mostly in silver set with amethysts, but some of gold, all of which had a clean, crisp quality that was highly sympathetic to the native materials used. A whole community of jewelers sprang up in Taxco around Spratling and his wife.

Though French designs were often slightly toned down for wealthy, conservative clients, several significant jewelry manufacturers like New York's Oscar Heyman & Brothers, the

Left: A design for a diamond and sapphire necklace, Oscar Heyman and Bros., c.1928.

Bonner Manufacturing Company, and Walter P. McTeigue, Inc. provided Saks Fifth Avenue and other exclusive department stores with their creations.

THE *MODERNE* EMBRACED

Even the mail-order Sears, Roebuck catalog featured *moderne* jewelry: diamond wedding rings in handsome geometric settings of platinum; bar pins and pendants featuring stepped designs; or watches boasting colored-paste embellishments. Of course, there were also American jewelers akin to Cartier (which had a New York branch, as did Van Cleef & Arpels and others). Some of them even had designs

Left: Cartier created this onyx and pavé-*set diamond pendant brooch with its pearl-scattered, detachable tassel. It represents a quintessentially* moderne *jewel.*

made up in Paris for them. In the main, precious American Art Deco *bijoux* tend to be more colorful than their Gallic counterparts.

THE DECLINE OF LUXURY

From 1930 the effects of the Depression were felt in luxury items. After the crash of 1929, and as the economic effects of the Depression deepened, firms were hesitant to produce new items which might prove difficult to sell.

Indeed, the 1925 Exposition had been the high point in Art Deco jewelry, accessories, and *objets d'art*. After this date, forms grew larger and more massive. Color was toned down until black and white predominated. The

Below: This 1930s' Tiffany & Co. brooch in the guise of a swordfish is made up of diamonds, emeralds, sapphires, and a ruby.

spirit of the period gradually faded and, with the advent of the Depression, the demand for luxury goods was severely reduced. The major jewelry houses cut back their staff or closed.

In 1935, Art Deco's grand master Georges Fouquet ceased major production. In the United States, Tiffany's remained open but operated with no additional staff. By this time the influence of the Bauhaus had been felt in all phases and spheres of the decorative arts. Industrial design, which was based on machine production, was assimilated into a design paradigm for the masses. The spirit of Art Deco had waned.

CHEAPER ALTERNATIVES
Geometric rings, clips, brooches, bracelets, lapel watches, and necklaces abounded, made from precious metals and jewels as well as of base metals or new alloys, paste, marcasite, plastic, and stones such as dark-red carnelian and apple-green chrysoprase – both chalcedonies and cheaper to use than the coral and jade that they resembled. Indeed, during the 1920s, the introduction of synthetic substances brought the price of artificial jewelry within the reach of the general population, and the Art Deco period therefore also spawned thousands of cheap, anonymous designs, many of which are now highly sought after by collectors today.

NEW MATERIALS
Art Deco costume jewelry, which was made out of base metals or silver set with marcasite, paste, or imitation stones, included bracelets, brooches, barrettes, and clips – for ears, shoes, lapels – in colored Bakelite, Celluloid, galalite and other synthetics, often in geometric shapes

Right: This French necklace, made of silver, paste and jade, dates from the mid-1920s.

or carved as stylized flowers.

COSTUME JEWELRY

During the 1920s and 1930s, costume jewelry, especially that with the imprimaturs of the trendsetting couturiers Coco Chanel – who championed the use of costume jewelry from the early 1920s – and Elsa Schiaparelli became ever more popular, outrageous and yet acceptable – from garish paste chokers and earrings to comical plastic-fish bangles, and (from Schiaparelli) a colored-metal, zodiac-sign necklace. Chanel especially utilized carved beads in her designs for imitation jewelry. Czechoslovakia, long a producer of glass beads, made inexpensive necklaces, pins and other bits of jewelry which were sometimes quite striking, with strong angles and colors.

AMUSING MOTIFS

The motifs of Art Deco costume jewels range from the sublime to the ridiculous: from stunning geometric configurations of paste to silly plastic cherries dangling from a wooden bar. The former borrowed its subject from *deluxe* jewelry of the time, but the latter – a joke – came about more or less on its own.

FIGURAL SUBJECTS

Unlike much of the jewelry in preceding eras, animals and people inhabited the world of 1920s' and 1930s' costume jewelry, from gentle silver fawns and playful plastic Scotty dogs to paste, turquoise, and marcasite Chinese men and elegant gilt-metal, cloche-hatted vamps. Flowers in every possible color, combination and variety sprouted on gilt-metal or silver

Right: This attractive set includes ear-clips, a necklace, and an expandable bracelet of gilt metal and casein, a type of plastic.

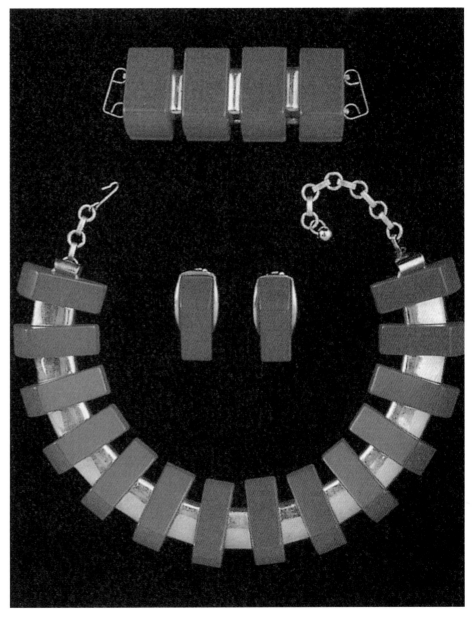

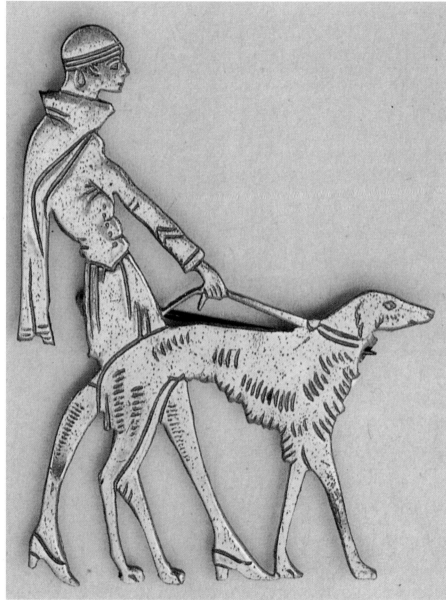

Above: This 1930s' silver deer pin is set with marcasites grouped to form patterns.

Left: An elegant lady walking her dog is the subject of this yellow-metal 1930s' brooch.

brooches and pendants, their paste petals glittering shamelessly.

During the late 1930s, however, sophisticated yet free-form designs began to appear (in both fine and costume jewelry, but especially the latter), with ribbons, bows, loops, and scrolls the predominant decorative motifs. The Napier and Coro companies in the U.S.A. were at the front of the manufacture of these so-called "cocktail jewels," which were highly kinetic and full of energy, unlike the more serene, decorative pieces of a decade or so earlier.

COSTUME JEWELRY REAPPRAISED
Art Deco costume jewelry – lovely, imaginative, fun, or all three – has surely come into its own in recent years. In its own time, the

Below: This airplane pin commemorates Charles Lindbergh's transatlantic flight.

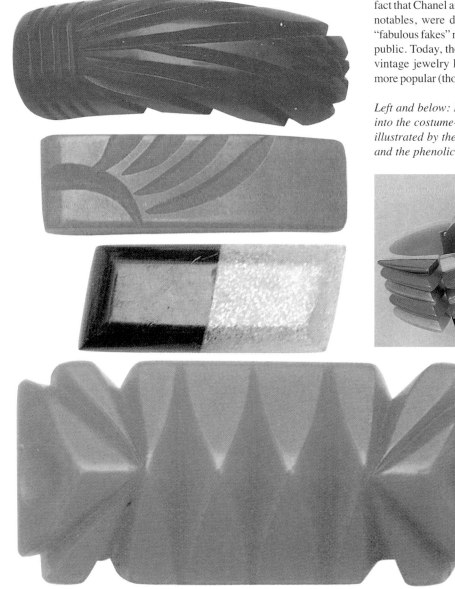

fact that Chanel and Schiaparelli, among other notables, were designing and sporting such "fabulous fakes" made them desirable to a wide public. Today, the rage for antique or recent-vintage jewelry has made these pieces even more popular (though less and less affordable).

Left and below: Plastics breathed new life into the costume-jewelry industry, as is illustrated by the clips and brooches, left, and the phenolic-resin bangles, below.